COME ON INTO THE RAIN FOREST

Written by Judy Nayer

MODERN CURRICULUM PRESS

PROJECT DIRECTOR: Susan Cornell Poskanzer
ART DIRECTOR: Lisa Olsson

MODERN CURRICULUM PRESS
13900 Prospect Road, Cleveland, Ohio 44136
Simon & Schuster • A Paramount Communications Company

This edition is published simultaneously in Canada by
Globe/Modern Curriculum Press, Toronto.

PHOTOGRAPHY CREDITS
Front Jacket:
© Paulette Brunner/Tom Stack & Associates p. 13 bottom; © John Chellman/Animals Animals pp. 8-9 bottom; © Ken Cole/Animals Animals p. 11 bottom; © Stephen Dalton/Animals Animals p. 12 top left; © David M. Dennis/Tom Stack & Associates p. 10 top inset; © Gerry Ellis/The Wildlife Collection p. 12 bottom; © Michael Fogden/Animals Animals p. 13 top right, p. 16 top right; © Michael Fogden, Oxford Scientific Films/Animals Animals p. 6, p. 9 bottom right, p. 10 center inset, p. 13 top left; © Mickey Gibson/Animals Animals p. 9 top; © G. C. Kelley/Tom Stack & Associates p. 9 center right; © Breck P. Kent/Animals Animals p. 14; © Gérard Lacz/Animals Animals p. 12 center left; © Tim Laman/The Wildlife Collection p. 3 background; © Richard K. LaVal/Animals Animals p. 12 top right; © Zig Leszczynski/Animals Animals p. 10 background, p. 11 center; © Raymond A. Mendez/Animals Animals p. 5 background; © Brian Parker/Tom Stack & Associates p. 15 background, p. 16 center left;© Partridge Productions Limited, Oxford Scientific Films/Animals Animals p. 7; © Don and Esther Phillips/Tom Stack & Associates p. 4; © Kevin Schafer/Tom Stack & Associates p. 8 top; © Kevin Schafer, Martha Hill/Tom Stack & Associates p. 16 center right; © Wendy Shattil, Bob Rozinski/Tom Stack & Associates p. 3 inset;© Dr. Nigel Smith/Animals Animals p. 5 inset; © Norbert Wu p. 15 inset

ILLUSTRATION CREDITS
© Susan Detrich, chart and map p. 16; © Martin Schneebalg, borders pp. 3-16 and inside front and back cover

ISBN 0-8136-1164-4 (STY PK) ISBN 0-8136-1165-2 (BB) ISBN 0-8136-1166-0 (SB)

10 9 8 7 6 5 4 3 2 96 95 94 93

COME ON INTO THE RAIN FOREST,
where animals roam free.
Come on into the rain forest,
there's so much life to see.

KEEL-BILLED TOUCAN

Shimmery blue butterflies
flutter in the breezes.
Hanging, dangling spider monkeys
swing from vine trapezes.

Howler monkeys screech and scream
and wake the day with sound.
Their calls stir forest families
for at least five miles around.

BLUE MOUNTAIN
SWALLOWTAIL BUTTERFLY

RED HOWLER MONKEYS
SPIDER MONKEYS

Shaggy sloths with long, curved claws
sleep upside-down with ease.
Babies cling to mothers' fur
and hide among the trees.

COME ON INTO THE RAIN FOREST,
where animals roam free.
Come on into the rain forest,
there's so much life to see.

Birds of every rainbow color
fly so light and free,
resting on leaves and branches
as they soar from tree to tree.

Toucans dance on perches
and look for food to eat.
They toss up nuts and berries
as they hang on by their feet.

Squawking, talking parrots
in reds and greens and blues
fill the forest with their
songs of danger, joy,
and news.

Hummingbirds with tiny wings
sip nectar just like bees.
The forest buzzes, hums, and sings
as they hover in the trees.

GREEN TREE PYTHON

GREEN PALM VIPER

WAGELS' VIPER

COME ON INTO THE RAIN FOREST,
where animals roam free.
Come on into the rain forest,
there's so much life to see.

RED-EYED TREE FROGS

Bright green snakes and lizards
move up and down the bark.
Choruses of red-eyed frogs
are heard from dawn to dark.

IGUANA

SHORT-TAILED
LEAF-NOSED FRUIT BAT
ANTHONY'S
FRUIT BAT
JAGUAR

Prowling, growling jaguars
wait to hunt at night.
In the forest darkness
furry bats take flight.

Beetles, ants, and centipedes
creep way down on the ground.
Everything is cool and wet–
there's darkness all around.

Anteaters flick their sticky tongues
and graze the forest floor.
In just one lick these giants catch
five hundred ants or more.

ANTEATER

COME ON INTO THE RAIN FOREST,
where animals roam free.
Come on into the rain forest,
there's so much life to see.

BASILISK LIZARD

RAIN FOREST FACTS

Rain forests are the greenest, warmest, wettest places in the world. The trees are always green. It is warm all year round, and it rains almost every day.

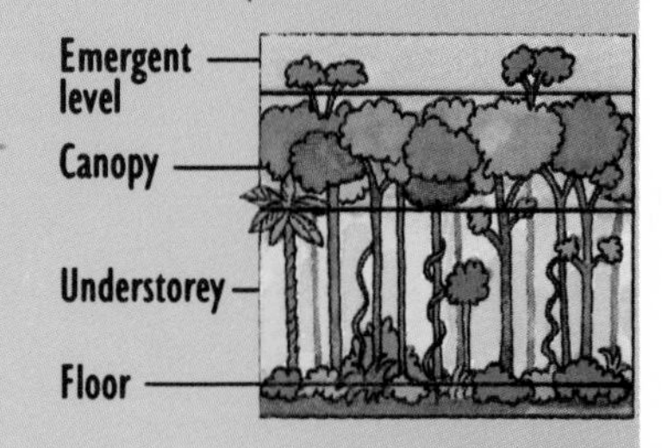

The levels of the rain forest from the top to the bottom are the emergent level, the canopy, the understorey, and the floor.

Rain forest plants give us many important medicines and cures.

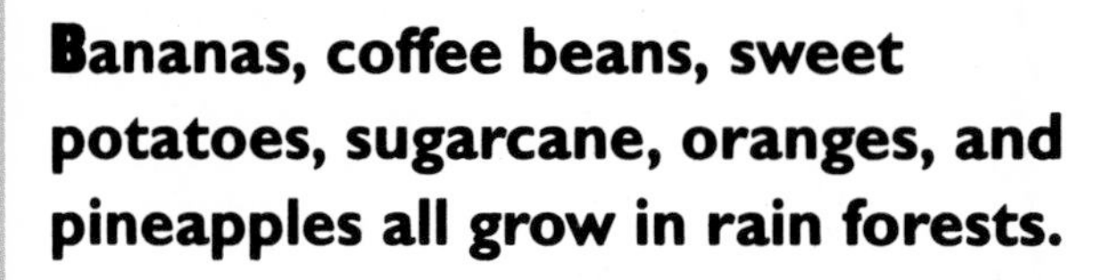

Bananas, coffee beans, sweet potatoes, sugarcane, oranges, and pineapples all grow in rain forests.

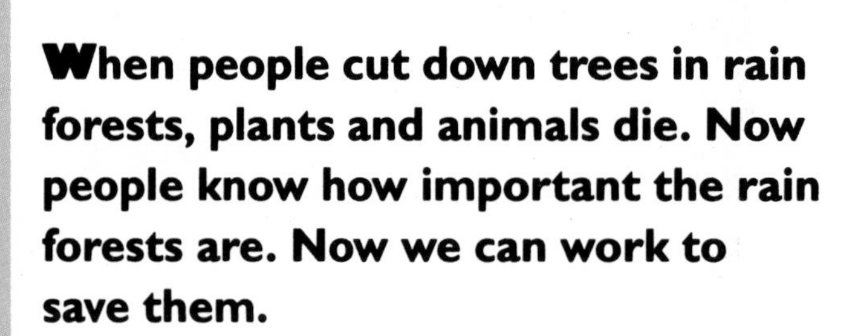

When people cut down trees in rain forests, plants and animals die. Now people know how important the rain forests are. Now we can work to save them.

There are rain forests all over the world. The rain forest in this book is in Central America.

■ = Rain forests